ALTERNATOR
BOOKS™

STATES OF MATTER

INVESTIGATIONS

KAREN LATCHANA KENNEY

Lerner Publications ◆ Minneapolis

To our future scientists and their unknown discoveries

Content Consultant: Dr. Neal D. Clements, Professional Engineer

Lerner Publications Company
A division of Lerner Publishing Group, Inc.
241 First Avenue North
Minneapolis, MN 55401 USA

For reading levels and more information, look up this title at www.lernerbooks.com.

Main body text set in Aptifer Slab Regular 11.5/18.
Typeface provided by Linotype AG.

Library of Congress Cataloging-in-Publication Data

Names: Kenney, Karen Latchana, author.
Title: States of matter investigations / Karen Latchana Kenney.
Description: Minneapolis : Lerner Publications, [2018] | Series: Key
    questions in physical science | Audience: Ages 8–12. | Audience:
    Grades 4 to 6. | Includes bibliographical references and index.
Identifiers: LCCN 2016050978 (print) | LCCN 2016054383 (ebook) |
    ISBN 9781512440065 (lb : alk. paper) | ISBN 9781512449600 (eb pdf)
Subjects: LCSH: Matter—Properties—Juvenile literature. | Physics—
    Juvenile literature.
Classification: LCC QC173.36 .K46 2018 (print) | LCC QC173.36
    (ebook) | DDC 530.4—dc23

LC record available at https://lccn.loc.gov/2016050978

Manufactured in the United States of America
1-42268-26125-4/3/2017

CONTENTS

PLUNGING IN

You step onto the pool's diving board. It bounces a little as you take a few steps forward. Right before you get to the edge, you jump up. You land on the board, and it launches you into the air. With arms up, you take a deep breath as you arc into the pool. Then you slice into the cool water.

Not only did you just complete a perfect dive, you also experienced several different states of matter. The hard board is a rigid solid. Your deep breath took in oxygen, a gas. And the

We experience matter in its different states all the time. Nearly everything around you is a solid, a liquid, or a gas.

Water is an important—and fun—substance. It has a solid form as well as a liquid form. And it can also be a gas!

cool water you dove into is a liquid. All three of these are made of matter.

Have you thought about why water can flow and freeze? Or why wood turns to ash when it's burned? Scientists wondered about these things too. When scientists have questions, they create theories and experiments to test their ideas. The evidence they find leads to conclusions, or answers about our world.

WHAT IS MATTER?

Everywhere you look, you'll see matter in its different states. It's in a raindrop as liquid, falling through the sky filled with gas. It's in a tree trunk or a snowflake as solids. It's even in you: all the many parts of your body are made of matter. In fact, everything in the universe is made of matter. If something has **mass** and takes up space, then it's matter.

Snowflakes are delicate and melt easily. But because they have a distinct shape, they are considered solids.

Democritus believed that atoms were all the same, but different shapes and positions of atoms made up different matter.

These states of matter seem very different, but they all have something in common. They are all made of tiny particles. Democritus was a Greek philosopher who lived about twenty-four hundred years ago. He believed all matter was made of particles he called **atoms**. He thought these atoms floated around and could also connect with other atoms using hooks. But Democritus had no way to prove his theory.

DISCOVERING ATOMS

In the early nineteenth century, British teacher and meteorologist John Dalton saw that water evaporates into air. He wondered how water and air could both be in the same space. But he thought that if water and air were

Dalton is sometimes called the father of chemistry. Unlike Democritus, Dalton believed that different matter is made up of different atoms. He set out to determine the different weights of each type of atom.

both made up of small particles, then these particles could mix during evaporation. By experimenting with mixtures of different gases, he determined that different gases are made from different kinds of small particles, or atoms.

MOLECULES IN MOTION

An individual atom is the smallest particle that can exist on its own. Atoms are always moving, even when they connect with other atoms. When two or more atoms combine, they make **molecules**. Molecules and atoms make up matter.

ARRANGEMENT OF ATOMS

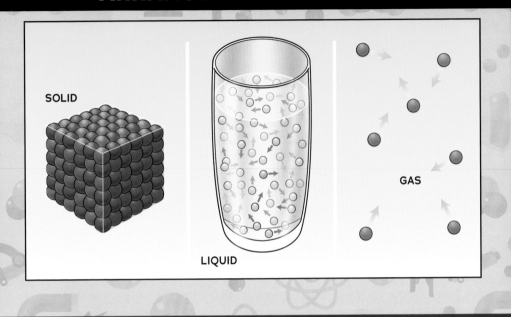

The atoms in solids are tightly packed together. There isn't much space for them to move around. That's what allows solids to keep their shape. A liquid's atoms are loosely connected, and they move around more than a solid's. This allows liquids to flow and take on the shape of their containers. In gases, atoms have lots of space between them. They fly in all directions and are just slightly connected. They fill up spaces of all sizes and have no shape.

Matter doesn't always stay the same, though—it can change from one state to another. Frost on the windows in the morning is the result of a gas turning into a solid.

Ice cream changes from a solid into a liquid when it becomes warm. This is an example of how temperature changes states of matter.

A frozen pond was a liquid that turned into a solid. And a sticky, melting ice-cream cone is a solid becoming a liquid. Temperature, **chemical reactions**, and pressure can all make matter change.

HOW DOES HEAT MELT ICE?

Have you ever seen a glass of ice water on a hot summer day? It doesn't take long for the ice to change. The cubes get smaller until they disappear completely. The solid ice slowly turns into liquid water in the glass.

Adding or removing heat is one way to make matter change its state. Just by observing nature, people knew that ice and snow melt when it is warm. But they didn't always know how that melting happened.

On a hot day, heat from the sun causes ice to melt. Melting happens when heat affects the atoms in a solid.

CHANGING SLOWLY

In the eighteenth century, scientists thought ice should become warm and immediately turn into liquid when heated to its **melting point**, 32°F (0°C). Instead, they saw that ice stayed cold as it was heated and only slowly melted. They wondered what happened to the heat when it's added to ice.

Scottish scientist Joseph Black investigated this problem in the 1750s. He experimented with two flasks of water. One had alcohol added, which prevents water from turning to ice. Black froze both flasks. Then he let both flasks warm up. The flask with alcohol warmed up by several degrees, but the other flask stayed at 32°F (0°C), even as the ice melted. Black thought that both flasks had absorbed the same amount of heat and concluded that heat is absorbed or released by matter when it changes states.

Black originally went to school to become a doctor, but he later became a professor of anatomy and chemistry. During this time, he began studying heat and temperature.

HEAT AND TEMPERATURE

During Black's time, many scientists didn't understand the difference between heat and temperature. They thought they were the same thing. Black's experiments with heat showed that it was very different from temperature. Heat is a form of energy, which is the ability to do work. Heat transfers between objects, such as ice in a glass of water. The ice and water soon have the same temperature, which is a measurement of how fast an object's molecules move.

So ice absorbs heat without changing temperature by turning into water. Since the flask with alcohol did not change states, it had a higher temperature.

CHANGING STATES

Heat is a form of energy. When ice melts, heat energy transfers into the ice, making its molecules move faster. They can't hold onto one another as easily and start breaking free. The water slowly changes from solid ice to flowing liquid water. With even more heat, the molecules would move much faster and turn into steam, a gas.

Snow and water are both made up of the same molecules. As the sun heats this snow, its molecules move faster, causing it to melt and drip off the branch as water droplets.

CHANGING WATER'S STATE WITH HEAT

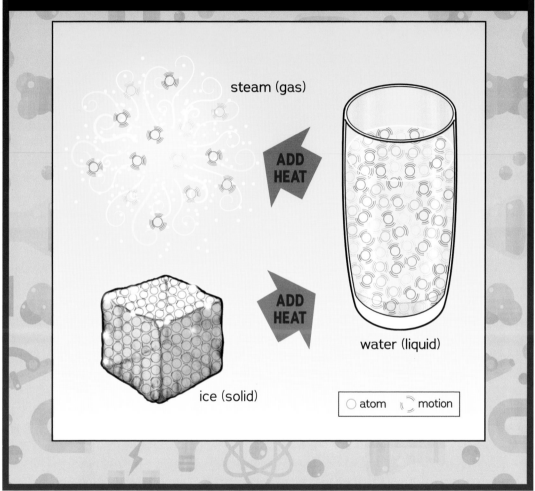

steam (gas)

ADD HEAT

water (liquid)

ADD HEAT

ice (solid)

○ atom   ◌ motion

By adding or removing heat, you can change matter's state. Yet the matter itself stays the same—ice and steam are still water. Its molecules just move faster or slower in its different states.

HOW DOES FIRE CHANGE WOOD?

It's a chilly fall night, and you're toasting marshmallows around a blazing campfire. Bright red flames reach up high as smoke trails into the sky. The wood below glows red, and some of it becomes white, powdery ash. What's happening to the wood?

A campfire is an example of a chemical reaction. In this case, the state of matter changes and so does the matter itself.

Ice can turn into water, then back into ice because the water molecules never change. But ash cannot turn back into wood because the molecules in wood break apart during the chemical reaction.

Early scientists wondered about this too. They did not understand why wood became ash when it burned. It seemed as if some of the wood's matter disappeared. These scientists thought that an invisible and mysterious substance they called phlogiston left the wood when it burned.

A NEW LAW

Then in the late eighteenth century, French chemist Antoine Lavoisier wanted to prove whether the phlogiston theory was true. For years, Lavoisier and other scientists conducted experiments on matter and **combustion**. Eventually Lavoisier came up with the law of conservation of mass. This law explains that matter can never be lost: it may change in form, but the total amount always stays the same.

If mass was never lost, Lavoisier believed phlogiston could not exist and wood must not actually be losing matter during a fire. In his experiments, Lavoisier burned substances such as phosphorous and sulfur. He found that when these substances burned, they actually gained mass. Oxygen combined with matter to make new products during the chemical reaction.

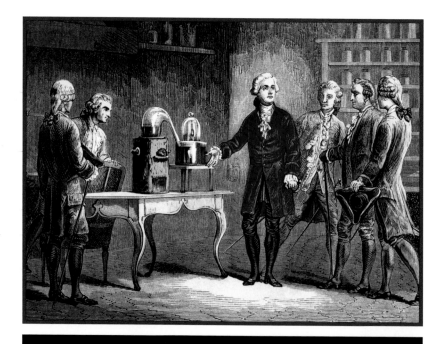

This artwork depicts Lavoisier *(center)* showing other scientists an experiment he used to isolate and name oxygen.

SCIENCE IN PRACTICE

In the late eighteenth century, Lavoisier and his wife, Marie-Anne, conducted several experiments to demonstrate the law of conservation of mass. In one experiment, they put fruit inside sealed glass containers, so that no matter could escape into the air. They weighed the container with fruit and then watched as the fruit rotted and broke down. When they weighed the container again, it had the same weight as it did at the beginning of the experiment, even though the matter inside looked very different.

Lavoisier used many different tools and instruments to conduct his experiments. This experiment combined oxygen and hydrogen to create water.

Extreme heat causes the hydrogen and carbon molecules in wood to vibrate so much that they eventually break apart. They quickly join with oxygen molecules instead to create carbon dioxide and water.

So when a campfire burns, oxygen molecules in the air combine with hydrogen and carbon molecules in the wood. This makes smoke, which contains carbon dioxide, a gas, and water vapor. The ash is the parts of the wood that won't burn up. If you weighed all of a fire's products, the weight would equal that of the wood before it burned.

CHAPTER 4

HOW DOES A FIRE EXTINGUISHER WORK?

Have you ever seen a carbon dioxide fire extinguisher in action? When someone presses on the nozzle, a huge jet of gas comes out of the small canister to put out a fire. But what exactly is happening?

Fire needs oxygen, fuel, and heat to burn. A carbon dioxide fire extinguisher removes both oxygen and heat to put out a fire.

UNDER PRESSURE

In the seventeenth century, British scientists Robert Boyle and Robert Hooke wanted to find out more about air. They experimented and found one more way to change states of matter: pressure. When increased pressure is applied to gases, they take up less space. Releasing that pressure allows gases to take up more space.

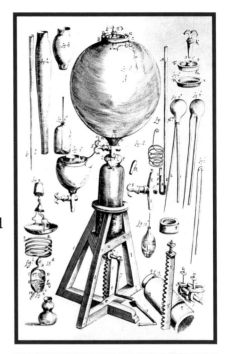

This drawing shows the air pump Hooke and Boyle built while experimenting with air pressure.

In the eighteenth century, Dutch scientist Martin van Marum wanted to test whether Boyle's experiment would also work with ammonia. As van Marum applied pressure to ammonia gas in a tube with **mercury**, the ammonia gas turned into a liquid. In the nineteenth century, British scientist Michael Faraday found that with increased pressure, he was able to turn carbon dioxide and other gases into small amounts of liquid too. Air pressure, water pressure, or pressure from a solid object surrounding the gas squeezes atoms closer together. The atoms begin to join together, turning gases into liquids.

SCIENCE IN PRACTICE

In the late 1650s, Boyle and Hooke began experimenting using a specially designed air pump and glass tubes. Boyle poured mercury into a j-shaped tube, trapping an air bubble at the short end. The bubble became smaller as he poured in more mercury, increasing pressure on the bubble. This showed that as the pressure increased, the gas took up less space. With less pressure, the gas bubble grew. Pressure could

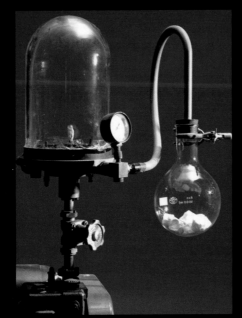

push a gas's molecules and atoms together. Boyle published the results of his experiment, which became known as Boyle's Law, in 1662.

This structure is used to demonstrate Boyle's Law. Marshmallows in the glass bulb (*right*) expand when pressure is reduced in the bulb.

Modern scientists can produce large amounts of liquid from gases using changes in pressure and temperature.

And pressure is what allows carbon dioxide fire extinguishers to hold such large amounts of gas. Inside a fire extinguisher's canister is a liquid form of carbon dioxide gas. When the pressure is released, the cold liquid shoots out as a gas. It also shoots out tiny pieces of ice. This gas quickly stops a fire from burning.

Gases always evenly fill the spaces they are in. In a fire extinguisher, a large amount of carbon dioxide gas is forced into the small space of the pressurized canister. But when the pressure is released, the gas is able to fill a bigger space, so it rushes quickly out of the extinguisher to spread evenly into its new space.

INSIDE A CARBON DIOXIDE FIRE EXTINGUISHER

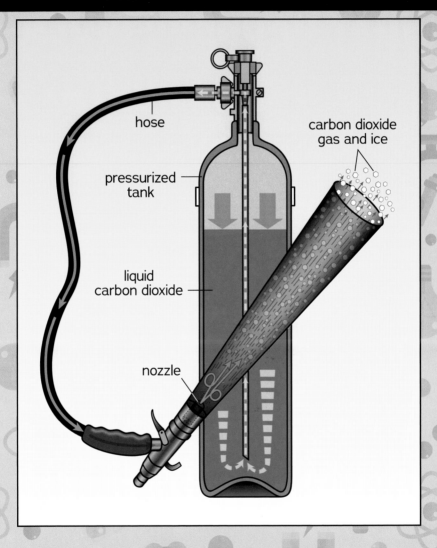

hose

carbon dioxide
gas and ice

pressurized
tank

liquid
carbon dioxide

nozzle

WHAT HAPPENS WHEN A VOLCANO ERUPTS?

It's hot deep below Earth's surface—hot enough to melt solid rock. This intense heat changes rock inside Earth into a liquid form called **magma** that moves and flows. The magma begins rising up above the solid rock, seeking an opening or a weak place in the surface of the Earth. This opening is known as a volcano.

The magma also contains gases, and as the magma rises, there is less pressure on it. The gases expand. When the

A volcano in Ecuador erupts in 2011.

magma reaches Earth's surface, the gases billow out into the sky. Soon the magma erupts as a fiery red liquid called lava. The lava spills down the side of the volcano and spreads out over the rocks. As it spreads, the lava cools down and hardens into a solid again, becoming shiny black volcanic rock.

An erupting volcano shows how temperature and pressure change matter from solids to liquids and back again. But matter in all its forms can be found all around us. Scientists continue to study how matter acts and changes. And what they learn through questions and experiments helps us understand our world.

Hardened black volcanic rock in Hawaii

TRY IT!

You've learned that matter can change through chemical reactions. Try this experiment to find out how a chemical reaction makes a solid react with a liquid inside a sandwich bag. Read through all the steps of the experiment. What do you think will happen to the bag?

❓ WHAT YOU'LL NEED

- 3 small ziplock plastic sandwich bags
- measuring cups
- cold, room temperature, and hot water
- vinegar
- teaspoon
- baking soda
- 3 tissues
- notebook
- pencil

❓ WHAT YOU'LL DO

1. Find a spot outside to do this experiment.
2. Pour ¼ cup of cold water and ½ cup of vinegar into a bag. Zip it halfway shut.
3. Measure 3 teaspoons of baking soda onto a tissue. Fold the tissue around it to make a ball.
4. Quickly add the tissue-baking soda ball to the bag and zip the bag. Put it on the ground and step back. Watch what happens and record what you see.

5. Try steps 2 to 4 again with the room temperature water and then hot water. After each try, record your observations.
6. Create a chart to clearly organize your data. Your chart should have spaces to explain and record the results of each round of your experiment.

❓ FOLLOW UP

Review your data to come up with your conclusions. Which bags expanded with gas? Which water temperature made the reaction happen the fastest? How did matter change in this experiment? How might heat, pressure, and chemical reactions work together in some cases to change states of matter?

atom: the smallest part of an element that has all the properties of that element

chemical reaction: a process by which two or more molecules interact and change into other molecules

combustion: the process of catching on fire and burning

magma: a mixture of melted rock and gases beneath Earth's surface

mass: the amount of matter in something

melting point: the temperature at which a solid melts. Water's melting point is 32°F (0°C).

mercury: a poisonous, silver-colored liquid metal

molecule: a group of atoms

LERNER

Expand learning beyond the printed book. Download free, complementary educational resources for this book from our website, www.lerneresource.com.

SOURCE

FURTHER INFORMATION

BBC Bitesize: Changing States
http://www.bbc.co.uk/bitesize/ks2/science/materials/changing_states/read/1/

The Changing State of Matter
http://eschooltoday.com/science/states-and-behaviour-of-matter/changing-states-of-matter.html

Changing States of Matter
http://www.chem4kids.com/files/matter_changes.html

Hanson-Harding, Alexandra. *What Is Matter?* New York: Britannica/Rosen, 2015.

Idaho Public Television: States of Matter—Facts
http://idahoptv.org/sciencetrek/topics/matter/facts.cfm

Ives, Rob. *Fun Experiments with Matter: Invisible Ink, Giant Bubbles, and More*. Minneapolis: Hungry Tomato, 2018.

Marsico, Katie. *Key Discoveries in Physical Science*. Minneapolis: Lerner Publications, 2015.

Winterberg, Jenna. *Conservation of Mass*. Huntington Beach, CA: Teacher Created Materials, 2016.

INDEX

PHOTO ACKNOWLEDGMENTS

The images in this book are used with the permission of: design elements: iDesign/Shutterstock.com; © iStockphoto.com/kotoffei. Suzanne Tucker/Shutterstock.com, p. 4; © iStockphoto.com/skynesher, p. 5; Jefunne/Shutterstock.com, p. 6; Masterpics/Alamy Stock Photo, p. 7; Photo Researchers, Inc/Alamy Stock Photo, p. 8; © Laura Westlund/Independent Picture Service, pp. 9, 15, 25; © iStockphoto.com/john shepherd, p. 10; © iStockphoto.com/TheCrimsonMonkey, p. 11; Georgios Kollidas/Shutterstock.com, p. 12; © iStockphoto.com/FLusvarghi, p. 13; © iStockphoto.com/maghakan, p. 14; © iStockphoto.com/omgimages, p. 16; vvoe/Shutterstock.com, p. 17; © Sheila Terry/Science Source, p. 18; © Print Collector/Hulton Archive/Getty Images, pp. 19, 22; Kimberly Shavender/Shutterstock.com, p. 20; © iStockphoto.com/georgeclerk, p. 21; © Andrew Lambert Photography/Science Source, p. 23; © iStockphoto.com/JonasSanLuis, p. 24; Ammit Jack/Shutterstock.com, p. 26; © John S Lander/LightRocket/Getty Images, p. 27.

Front cover: © nikkytok/Shutterstock.com.